MOBOB8MNM

mmm8080om

A Sense of Science:
Exploring Light

Claire Llewellyn

SEA-TO-SEA
Mankato Collingwood London

This edition first published in 2009 by
Sea-to-Sea Publications
Distributed by Black Rabbit Books
P.O. Box 3263
Mankato, Minnesota 56002

Printed in China

Library of Congress
Cataloging-in-Publication Data:

Llewellyn, Claire.
  Exploring light / Claire Llewellyn.
      p. cm. -- (A sense of science)
  Summary: "A simple exploration of light that
covers sunlight, electrical lights, shadows, and
how animals and plants need light to live. Includes
activities"--Provided by publisher.
  Includes index.
  ISBN 978-1-59771-130-2
  1. Light--Juvenile literature. I. Title.
  QC360.L554 2009
  535--dc22
                        2008007330

9 8 7 6 5 4 3 2

Published by arrangement with
the Watts Publishing Group Ltd,
London.

Editor: Jeremy Smith
Art Director: Jonathan Hair
Design: Matthew Lilly
Cover and design concept:
Jonathan Hair
Photography: Ray Moller unless
otherwise stated.

Photograph credits:
Alamy: 10b, 25t,
Corbis: 6, 11t, 13b, 17b.

We would like to thank Scallywags for their help
with the models in this book.

Contents

A light in the sky

In the morning
the Sun rises.
It gives us light.

Sunlight lets us see the world.

Clouds can cover the Sun.

Under a cloud
What changes do you see and feel when the Sun goes behind a cloud?

Light in our home

At night, the sky gets dark. Electric lamps help us see.

A flashlight is a little electric lamp.

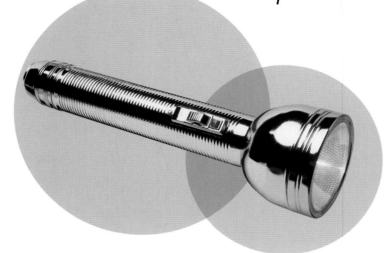

Flashlight!
Hide under a blanket with a flashlight. How do you turn it on and off? What happens when you do?

We need light in all sorts of places!

Light and heat

Most things that give out light also give out heat.

Warning!
We need to be careful with hot things.

Hot and cold

Take some ice cream out of the freezer and taste it. Then leave it in the sun for five minutes and taste it again. What is different?

In the summer, the sun is very hot. Staying in the shade protects our skin.

Sun lotion can also help stop our skin from burning.

We see with light

We need light to see the world around us. Our eyes cannot see in the dark.

Can you see?

What can you see out of the kitchen window in the daytime? What can you see when it's dark?

We make a room darker by blocking out light.

Without natural light we need help to see things clearly.

Our eyes

We have two eyes on our face.
Our eyes have different parts.

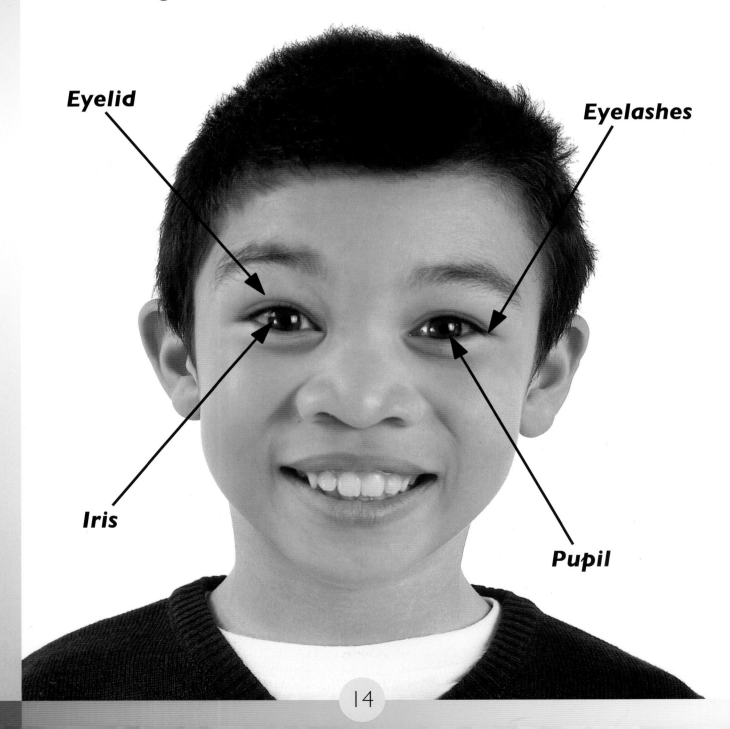

Eyelid

Eyelashes

Iris

Pupil

Eye watch

Keep your eyes open but cover them with your hands. Then uncover them. What happens?

Bright light can hurt our eyes.

A cap protects our eyes from the Sun. So do sunglasses.

Feeling our way

It's hard to get around in the dark. It helps if we can feel with our hands.

Our fingers help tell us where we are.

Touchy feely

Shut your eyes. Ask a friend to pass you some things. Can you feel what they are?

This person cannot see. He is feeling his way with a stick.

Animals at night

Many animals hunt in the dark.

An owl's big eyes help it see in the dark.

A fox finds prey at night using its nose and ears.

A bat's sharp ears help it catch insects.

Shadows

If we stand outside on a sunny day, our body makes a shadow on the ground.

Shadows are made when something blocks the Sun's rays.

In the shade

On a sunny day, stand in the shadow of a tree. Does it feel any different from standing in the sun?

When the Sun is low in the sky, shadows are at their longest.

An electric light makes shadows, too.

Shadows change

When we move,
our shadow
moves too.

It changes in all sorts of ways.

Shadow play
Make an animal shadow
with your hands. Now
make your animal move.

When the puppet
is near an electric
light, its shadow
is big.

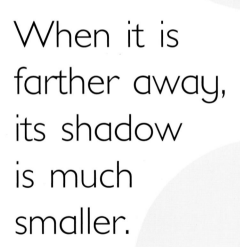

When it is
farther away,
its shadow
is much
smaller.

smooth and shiny

Some things are smooth and shiny.

Light makes them stand out brightly.

Mirror, mirror

Touch a mirror. What does it feel like? What happens when you shine a flashlight on it?

The mirror sparkles in the candlelight.

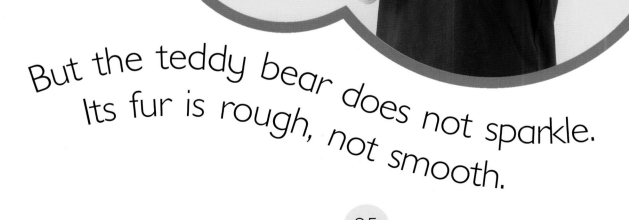

But the teddy bear does not sparkle. Its fur is rough, not smooth.

Light and life

Plants need light
to grow and survive.

Without light

With light

They don't grow properly in the dark.

Cover up

Cover a leaf on a potted plant with some foil. After a week remove the foil. What can you see?

Without plants, there would be nothing for this rabbit to eat.

Without plants, and the animals that eat them, there would be nothing for us to eat either!

Glossary

Cloud
A mass of tiny water drops floating in the sky.

Electric
Worked by electricity.

Electricity
A kind of power that gives us light.

Flashlight
A small light we can carry around.

Iris
The colored part of the eye.

Lamp
A machine that gives out light.

Pupil
A hole in the eye that lets light pass through. It looks like a black dot.

Shadow
The shape made when something blocks out light.

Shade
A place where the Sun cannot reach.

Sun
The hot, bright star close to the Earth.

Make a black box

1. Find an empty box and line it with black paper.

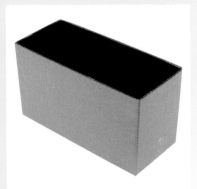

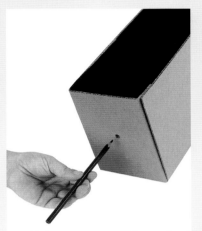

2. Make a tiny peephole in one end of the box.

3. Make a larger hole in the lid and cover it with cardboard.

4. Put a few things inside the box.

5. Ask a friend to look through the peephole. What can they see in the box?

6. Let in a little more light by moving the cardboard cover. What can be seen through the peephole now?

Index